Connecting Comprehension Strategies to the Urban Student

Through Conversations and Analogies

Engaging Beginnings
(Mini-Lessons that set the tone for Learning)

Annika Hardy-Douglas

authorHOUSE®

AuthorHouse™
1663 Liberty Drive
Bloomington, IN 47403
www.authorhouse.com
Phone: 1 (800) 839-8640

Published by AuthorHouse 04/20/2016

ISBN: 978-1-5246-0424-0 (sc)
ISBN: 978-1-5246-0423-3 (e)

Library of Congress Control Number: 2016906343

Investigative Circle

The idea of the investigative circle mimics the concept of a literature circle. The purpose of the investigative circle is to explore informational text, complex text, and non-fiction text in a more intimate way. Students are expected to conduct several close reads in order to completely understand the reading material. Students will also have individual jobs to complete with the expectation of sharing out in a collaborative setting.

JOBS

Questioner: As the **Questioner**, your job is to generate questions that can be answered through careful investigation. It is wise to form your questions before you read **(Based on the Title)** during the reading **(Based on what you are thinking)** and after you have read **(Based on what you're still wondering about)**

Predictor: As the predictor, your job is to closely read the text and periodically stop to think. Make predictions on what you think may happen next, what the next paragraph may be about, or what you think the outcome of an event may be. Write at least 3 predictions with evidence that will support each one. Share your predictions with your group members.

Data Collector: As the data collector your job is to accurately record pieces of text that made you want to stop and think, question, reflect, or make logical inferences. Read each piece of text to your group members and discuss why you feel the information/data that you collected is valuable and important for understanding the text.

Analyzer: As the analyzer your job is to examine the details of the text very closely. Conduct a close read of the text. You may highlight, underline, annotate, and "tag the text" as much as possible to gain a strong understanding of what you have read. Write a paragraph that is a conclusion of your thinking. Use evidence from the text to support your conclusion or final analysis.

Questioner

As the **Questioner**, your job is to generate questions that can be answered through careful investigation. It is wise to form your questions before you read **(Based on the Title)** during the reading **(Based on what you are thinking)** and after you have read **(Based on what you're still wondering about)**

Below are some sample Question Starters:

Who?

Where?

Which one?

What?

How?

Why?

How much?

How many?

When?

What does this mean?

Which are the facts?

Write in your own words ...

How would you explain ...?

Write a brief outline ...

What do you think could have happened next?

Who do you think...?

What was the main idea ...?

Clarify why ...

Illustrate the ...

Write at least 5 questions you can share with your group. Discuss possible answers, and use **evidence** to support your answers.

1.

2.

3.

4.

5.

Predictor

As the predictor, your job is to closely read the text and periodically stop to think. Make predictions on what you think may happen next, what the next paragraph may be about, or what you think the outcome of an event may be. Write at least 3 predictions with evidence that will support each one. Share your predictions with your group members.

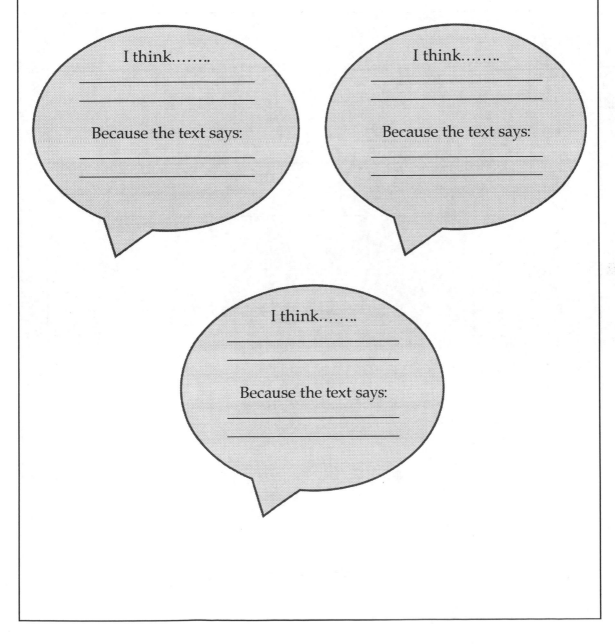

Data Collector

As the data collector your job is to accurately record pieces of text that made you want to stop and think, question, reflect, or make logical inferences. Read each piece of text to your group members and discuss why you feel the information/ data that you collected is valuable and important for understanding the text.

Analyzer

As the data collector your job is to accurately record pieces of text that made you want to stop and think, question, reflect, or make logical inferences. Read each piece of text to your group members and discuss why you feel the information/ data that you collected is valuable and important for understanding the text.

Contents

Acknowledgements

This book is really a diary of lesson plans. Each lesson plan was created to hook students, to get them interested, and to encourage them to want to continue learning how to think when they read. The outcome of anything you love doing will always be great each and every time. Passion is not only seen, it is felt as well. Children are like sponges that soak up all types of energy. That is why I love them so much. They are not yet flawed by conformity, and in a great classroom environment are allowed to be themselves, to think like they are wired to think, to argue, to debate, to prove their way of thinking by what they feel is true. In my classroom environment children are free to be delicately abrasive with the intent of sharing their minds with others and being heard, but even more important, being accepted.

In order for me to reach my students I have to become a student myself. I have to not conform to what a teacher is "supposed" to look like, sound like, or act like. I have to be as transparent as I want my students to be with me. Children need to know and understand that you are just as human as they are. You should be comfortable sharing yourself as the imperfect being you are in a non-intimidating way. Students have the right to know that as a teacher you don't have all of the answers to everything, and that each day is a new learning experience for you as well. When children feel welcomed in the classroom they will begin to feel comfortable enough to let down their guard down, or the walls they some students tend to have up. Although, most of the more challenging students would never admit it, they really do want a teacher to care enough to knock their wall down. It truly does take an artist to knock down walls, character build, inspire, motivate, love, care, and teach. This is a job that requires patience, transparency, a will to give, a desire to learn, and a growth mindset. You are a gifted and special person as an educator, because everyone can 't do this job well!

I would like to dedicate this book to all of the children I have ever had the pleasure of working with. My son Mekhi and my daughter Mackenzie! I want my children to know how important education is, and how it should be valued at all times. There were fearless people who came before us, stripped of the right to be educated, but they fought for future generations to be able to learn. That is why education is important and is the most powerful tool you can use to achieve greatness in your life. A well-educated mind is a free mind. I would also like to extend this dedication to three powerful principals that have made a positive influence on my teaching abilities. Thank you Jonnie Nelson, Toni Young, and Tammie Bolden. All three of these ladies are phenomenal African-American leaders, mentors, and coaches in the field of education. As a quiet observer I was able to pick up many valuable things to incorporate in my line of work. Through these ladies, my confidence was enhanced, I was encouraged to further myself academically, and more importantly I learned how to think as a professional woman in the field of education. These are jewels that are rarely shared between women and I appreciate them so dearly.

A special thank you to my cousin Tamara Bailiff-Brown who taught me how to read and write as a kid, to my sister Shanell Allen-Debela who modeled for me the importance of education. I became motivated with the college tours she took me on as a teenager, and those experiences have helped me make some wise decisions in my academic career. Love you sis! Mom! You're the greatest, most talented woman I have ever known. You've always made any type of work look so easy. I know you are living your dream of becoming a teacher vicariously through me. I'm so lucky to have inherited your creativity and wisdom, and even more lucky to have you as my mother.

"The only trend I wish to set is the one that leaves my children educated and financially sound."

Prelude

My reality is that I have been destined to touch the lives of our youth. This destiny does not discriminate against any race, economic class, gender, or social status. This destiny invites any child into a fair place where learning can be achieved as a partnership. However, being that I am a minority teacher I am especially interested and invested in providing students from all different walks of life, those that are also of the minority exposure to real world situations that they may not have been given the opportunity to experience in their home environment.

The field of education faces numerous challenges as educators attempt to embrace the "new generation" of urban youth. The truth is most kids that spawn from "Urban" America are too concerned with popular trends. To them spending six plus hours in school is futile, they would much rather be engaged in some type of technological device, music, dance, or the slew of other creative art forms that take their attention off of classroom instruction. When you combine that with their misconception of teachers only teaching for a paycheck, and the idea that teachers don't really care if their students learn or not, you end up with an over-populated, under-educated society of "could-have beens." Our urban clientele is a melting pot of minority students. These students are bored with traditional teaching practices. They need someone to tap into their creative minds in order to keep their attention. This can only be achieved when teachers are willing to utilize professional development opportunities that are geared towards learning about cultural differences, healthy ways to build relationships among diverse students, and the importance of children being exposed to a wide range of multi-cultural literature. Not only should this literature be explored, but it should also be included in each classroom library for the diversity among the students you service.

Unfortunately, not every child will have the pleasure of receiving education from a teacher that looks like them. However, teachers do have the power to become culturally aware in order to build respectful and caring relationships with their students who are from a different cultural background than their own. If the investment is made, not only will every type of child gravitate to that "master teacher," but they will also begin to understand how the world is designed to function as it relates to compassion for all, even for those that we don't quite understand.

With every success there will be a challenge. White teachers tend to be the most dominant in the education field. Their jobs can become very tricky when they are put into situations that they are not familiar with. This includes becoming a teacher and a mentor for the diverse student. Teachers may become discouraged when trying to reach the diverse students in their classrooms. These frustrations will soon cause some teachers to give up on those children. They then decide to do the bare minimum for those children for the sake of avoiding confrontation that could be directly attributed to cultural differences, and unintentionally disrespecting the family. There should be no barriers in education, especially when the ultimate goal is for learning to take place. A teacher must accept the fact that in order to become a **GREAT** educator, he or she must also take on the role of "researcher." Nobody will ever be able to fully understand anything that they don't take the time to study. This includes our urban youth! You'd be surprised to see how fast these kids can rise to a challenge! Generation Z students possess competitive spirits that will motivate them to learn whatever is put before them. When instruction is authentic and meaningful you will witness the genius come out of each child. The bar should never be lowered because of what the teacher doesn't understand; instead the teacher has to, by any means necessary, find a way to tap into the minds of each type of child, and every kind of student. That is when real learning begins and this is when understanding can be appreciated on many different levels.

Motivation to me is one of the most important factors needed to successfully reach our urban youth. Many teachers are over-worked and underpaid for the amount of work that they are required/expected to do. In order for children to become motivated, the teacher must be excited first. Emotions have the power to travel from one vessel to another. If the mothership is unloading negative energy, there is no way on earth students will become enthusiastic about learning. Anyone who has truly taught knows that a teacher's job doesn't begin or end with a curriculum guide. A passionate educator wears many hats. Most of the time we don't even realize when we're shifting from teacher to counselor, to doctor, to mentor, to parental figure, to even a friend. The ability to switch roles in a professional way becomes natural and even habitual to those who are truly invested. With that being stated, teaching is not for everyone! The bible even states in James 3:1, "Not many of you should become teachers, my brothers, for you know that we who teach will be judged with greater strictness." My interpretation of that verse is that when you know better, you should do better. To me, that means becoming whomever or whatever you need to become in order to convey meaningful and authentic learning opportunities for students to grow by. This collection of lesson plans is not by any means a professional book of literature that highlights research based strategies that are known to promote academic achievement or growth. Instead, this collection was created to give those teachers who may be struggling with motivation from their students a little hope. All of the lesson plans included in this booklet should be used to introduce skills. These are the "attention getters" for each reading comprehension skill. After introducing the skill, teachers still have the freedom of following their curriculum guides, adding or taking away from lessons, or exploring more creative outlets that may help build motivation for learning and differentiate instruction.

I invite you into my classroom! I invite you into our conversations as they relate to comprehension strategies and the real world! Each strategy is introduced creatively, to spark an interest. The way a teacher chooses to tweek each lesson should be dependent on the classroom makeup.

What is comprehension?

Every attempt to define comprehension will offer certain uniqueness. There are many complicated things to consider when one is trying to build meaning. The ways in which understanding takes place are probably just as unique as a persons fingerprint. To me, comprehension is the outcome of your experiences and your ability to connect it to present day. My perception of comprehension is something like poetry. It is an intimate relationship between the reader and the text. It is an exchange of emotions, a trust, and a reliable validation of understanding for the reader. Each interpretation is a strand of a person's experience, and no strand is the same. Therefore, the way we construct meaning is based on the impact our experiences left on us. As people we may have had some of the same experiences, but no two experiences are exactly the same because everyone receives messages differently. Since comprehension is closely related to experience and prior-knowledge we can conclude that no matter how similar students work to construct meaning, each interpretation will offer an individual anomaly.

A healthy concept of teaching comprehension strategies should include explicit instruction. This type of instruction encourages students to become habitual thinkers. Students need to be taught how to think in order to be actively engaged in a text. If one of the expectations in your classroom is to hold students accountable for their understanding by proving their thinking, you're actually training students to lean on the text as well as themselves to build an authentic relationship with the text.

The stages involved in explicit teaching and learning should include: introduction, modeling, guided instruction, partnered learning, independent work, and reflection. Each of these components suggests a give and take relationship. In the beginning you give the students what they need to know in order to become successful. The giving should provide students with an opportunity to gain ownership over the strategy that they're working on, a creative way to model the strategy gives the teacher the opportunity to spark their interest, guided instruction and partnered learning builds confidence, independent work allows students to apply their knowledge, and reflections gives students the opportunity to examine their strengths and weaknesses. This type of instruction really mimics the principles that are based on the gradual release of responsibility (Fisher & Frey, 2008). What does that look like exactly?

Introduction:

- Introduce the strategy/skill
- Connect it to life with an analogy
- Create a visual artifact with the students so that they gain ownership over their learning

- Ask essential questions to spark a brief discussion

Model:

- Choose a high-interest book to read aloud while modeling the skill/strategy you are teaching
- Think aloud while reading in order to include students in the story, keep their attention by asking questions
- Apply the skill to a big sheet of paper that could be used as a graphic organizer so that students have a visual to refer back to
- Discuss the end product as a whole group

Guided Instruction:

- Students attempt to apply the strategy with assistance from teacher
- Strategy is modeled, but in a partnership that includes the students, and builds confidence
- Teacher should continuously provoke thought by providing questions, giving cues, and scaffolding learning so that students feel successful

Partnered Learning:

- Students get the opportunity to monitor their own learning/progress
- Students feel more comfortable learning and sharing ideas with their peers; collaborative learning helps build confidence
- Students are exposed to different perspectives which builds schema for those that need it

Independent:

- Students apply their knowledge to complete a task without assistance
- Students use graphic organizers to plot thinking

Reflection:

- Students complete a reflection paragraph recalling important details needed to successful use the strategy/skill
- Students complete an exit slip that connects their learning to real life and shows the benefits

Curriculum guides and district expectations for student learning usually put a time table on what a student should have learned by a certain date. In my opinion, this robs the teacher of their individual creativity, and rushes students through multiple processes needed to grasp learning. However, an engaging and authentic introduction to any concept or strategy could set the tone for even what pacing guides have to offer.

Students of all kinds love order. Although, there is a great possibility that they may resist it in the beginning because it's unfamiliar to them, the more consistent the method of your instruction is delivered, the more it becomes appreciated by students who need that order in order to become successful.

CCSS.ELA-Literacy.RL.6.10
CCSS.ELA-Literacy.SL.6.1
Skill: Predicting

Grade Level: 5th-9th

Analogy: Expectations!

Conversation: The person who knows you or the person that you know the best is probably your mom and dad! For some of you the person who knows you the best is your caregiver, basically whomever takes good care of you. Therefore, you have over time learned each other's behaviors. You can kind of "expect" how those people would react in certain situations. A "prediction" is just like that. You form a prediction based on what you already know in your head, and that why you expect or guess something will happen the way you think it would.

Example: If it is raining outside and you need to go outside, I would expect you to grab an umbrella or raincoat before you went out in the rain. Because I knew in my head that rain is wet, and most people don't like to get wet by rain I can "expect" or "guess" that you would grab some rain protection. That is how you predict!

Essential Question: Why is it helpful to make predictions in life and while you read?

~ On a large sheet of paper pose the essential question. Distribute 2 sticky notes to each student and allow them to answer the question on each sticky note. Allow 5 minutes to pass.

Share: Allow students to share their thinking with the closest friend, and report out whole group upon your discretion. Post sticky notes on the large sheet of white paper and post it on the classroom wall as an artifact for future use.

Model: Model the reading strategy while reading a trade book of your choice occasionally stopping to involve students in making predictions.

Independent Reflection: Have students reflect on the use of the skill alone. Students can write a short paragraph that elaborates on the essential question. Responses should include how this skill is beneficial in life and while reading! Responses should be used as an informal assessment, a teacher may choose to revisit and reteach parts of the lesson based on their findings.

CCSS.ELA-Literacy.SL.6.1
CCSS.ELA-Literacy.RL.6.1
CCSS.ELA-Literacy.RL.6.10
Skill: Inference

Grade Level: 5th-9th

Analogy: Human Emotions!

Conversation: Act out a human emotion. This emotion can be sad, happy, angry, excited, etc! Whichever you choose you must be able to act it out well! After you act out the emotion, ask students to identify what type of mood you are in. This will prompt students to raise their hands in order to give you feedback! Once a few students have identified your mood, extend the question with another one. Based on what you know about my mood, what type of day do you think I'll have? When students answer the last question, inform them that they have just made an inference!

Example: Tell students that an inference and a prediction are like cousins! They are related, but very different. With a prediction you guess what will happen next, or what you expect to happen next. With an inference you combine what you already know about something with any information you were given! That makes your guess an educated one based off of evidence! Explain to students that looking at pictures, facial expressions, or while reading can make an inference!

Essential Question: Why is it important for a person to make inferences in life and while reading?

~ On a large sheet of paper pose the essential question. Distribute 2 sticky notes to each student and allow them to answer the question on each sticky note. Allow 5 minutes to answer questions and discuss.

Inference

10-9-13

  An inference and a prediction
are like cousins. They are related,
but are different.
  Making an inference means you combine
the information in the text, with your own
thinking in order to make an educated guess!
    Other ways to say it:
- Infer
- drawing conclusions
- an educated guess
- "reading between the lines"

You can infer while reading, listening or looking
at illustrations/pictures

CCSS.ELA-Literacy.RL.6.2
CCSS.ELA-Literacy.RL.6.3
CCSS.ELA-Literacy.RL.6.10
CCSS.ELA-Literacy.SL.6.1
Skill: Summarizing

Grade Level: 5th-9th

Analogy: Remembering stuff that matters to you!

Conversation: Have you ever been to a place and had the greatest time of your life there? Or, Have you ever been to a place and had the worse time of your life there? And, you can remember each detail of that time just like it happened yesterday! If you can remember and can tell it or write it, you are giving a summary!

Example: Teacher shares a personal event in which he/she recalls all of the most important parts. This may include: plot, rising action, climax, falling action, resolution, etc. After the story is told, the teacher can highlight all of the components shown on a plot diagram, and how they should be included in a retell summary or a written summary!

Essential Question: Why is it important for a person to be able to recall events from their life and after reading?

Share: Allow students to share their thinking with the closest friend, and report out whole group upon your discretion. Post sticky notes on the large sheet of white paper and post it on the classroom wall as an artifact for future use.

Model: Model the reading strategy while reading a trade book of your choice! Upon finishing the story allow students to respond to summarizing graphic organizer that highlights the most important parts of a story.

Independent Reflection: Have students reflect on the use of the skill alone. Students can write a short paragraph that elaborates on the essential question. Responses should include how this skill is beneficial in life and while reading! Responses should be used as an informal assessment, a teacher may choose to revisit and reteach parts of the lesson based on their findings.

Essential Question:

How can I summarize a text only using the important pieces of information?

A summary is a retell of a story that includes only the important parts. Parts of a good retell will include: Exposition(beginning) Rising Action (what leads to the problem) Climax(most exciting part) Falling Action (how problem is solved) Resolution(end)

Annika Hardy-Douglas

CCSS.ELA-Literacy.RL.6.10
CCSS.ELA-Literacy.SL.6.1
Skill: Cause and Effect

Grade Level: 5th-9th

Analogy: For every action there will be a reaction!

Conversation: From the moment you wake up in the morning until the time you rest your head down to sleep at night you are living out cause and effect relationships. For every action that you make there will be a reaction. Sometimes one initial action can lead to multiple reactions. That is cause and effect! The cause of a situation is why it happens and the effect is what happens as a result of the cause.

Example: Most people use an alarm clock to wake up for work, school, or important engagements. The cause is setting the alarm clock. The effect is waking up when you hear the buzzer go off. The word "because" is a signal word that you should always use to identify the cause of a situation. Because the alarm clock went off, the effect is that you wake up! (Other examples can be used to show the cause and effect relationship)

Essential Question: How can cause and effect relationships help you make good choices in life?

Share: Allow students to share their thinking with the closest friend, and report out whole group upon your discretion. Post sticky notes on the large sheet of white paper and post it on the classroom wall as an artifact for future use.

Model: Model the reading strategy while reading a trade book of your choice! Upon finishing the story allow students to respond to a cause and effect graphic organizer that highlights the why and the what of given situations.

Independent Reflection: Have students reflect on the use of the skill alone. Students can write a short paragraph that elaborates on the essential question. Responses should include how this skill is beneficial in life and while reading! Responses should be used as an informal assessment, a teacher may choose to revisit and reteach parts of the lesson based on their findings.

Culminating Activity: *Allow students to split up into groups and act out short skits that show cause and effect relationships. When students present skits whole group, those watching can identify the cause and the effect on sticky notes, and reveal their findings out loud, before the next group presents their skit.*

CCSS.ELA-Literacy.RL.6.3
CCSS.ELA-Literacy.RL.6.5
CCSS.ELA-Literacy.RL.6.10
CCSS.ELA-Literacy.SL.6.1
Skill: Analyzing

Grade Level: 5th-9th

Analogy: The mad scientist!

Conversation: There are actual people in life that get paid big money to apply a skill that good readers use every day to understand that they are reading! They get paid to analyze people, situations, evidence, and books!

Example: In order for a scientist to completely understand the specimen that he places under the microscope he has to examine it very closely. When a detective has to explain a crime scene, he has to analyze it! When you analyze you look at things very closely and carefully in order to make sense of it, to understand it better! (Other examples can be used to spark the student's attention)

Essential Question: How can being able to analyze be helpful in life and while reading?

Share: Allow students to share their thinking with the closest friend, and report out whole group upon your discretion. Post sticky notes on the large sheet of white paper and post it on the classroom wall as an artifact for future use.

Model: Model the reading strategy while reading a trade book of your choice! Draw attention to the main character of the story. Tell students that you will analyze the main character and based on the evidence in the text you will give that character traits. Each character trait should be based on dialogue, or actions that the main character has made.

Independent Reflection: Have students reflect on the use of the skill alone. Students can write a short paragraph that elaborates on the essential question. Responses should include how this skill is beneficial in life and while reading! Responses should be used as an informal assessment, a teacher may choose to revisit and reteach parts of the lesson based on their findings.

Culminating Activity: Have students self-select their own trade book. Each student will independently read a leveled book, analyze the main character, and create a character sketch that may include character traits based on evidence from the story!

Ron's Character Trait's
Smart
Brave
Outgoing
Respectful
Nice

CCSS.ELA-Literacy.SL.6.1
CCSS.ELA-Literacy.RL.6.10
Skill: Evaluation

Grade Level: 5th-9th

Analogy: A Judge and Jury

Conversation: An evaluator considers a situation and makes a judgment based on the evidence or information that is presented. When you evaluate something you are actually combining several reading skills at once in order to make a reasonable evaluation.

Example: A judge evaluates a case that is heard in a court of law. In order for the judge to make a fair and reasonable evaluation he/she must consider all of the evidence or information presented. A jury does the same exact thing. However, the jury must come to an agreement before they can present their verdict. The jury collects information and analyzes it, makes inferences, and evaluates. Whatever the outcome is after thorough evaluation is the judgment.

Essential Question: Why is it important to evaluate a situation, circumstance, or information before you make a judgment?

Share: Allow students to share their thinking with the closest friend, and report out whole group upon your discretion. Post sticky notes on the large sheet of white paper and post it on the classroom wall as an artifact for future use.

Model: Show a video clip of students around the same grade level having a debate, or an argument. Select a student evaluator who will listen and consider both sides of the argument. After careful consideration the evaluator makes a decision on who wins the debate.

Independent Reflection: Have students reflect on the use of the skill alone. Students can write a short paragraph that elaborates on the essential question. Responses should include how this skill is beneficial in life and while reading! Responses should be used as an informal assessment, a teacher may choose to revisit and reteach parts of the lesson based on their findings.

CCSS.ELA-Literacy.SL.6.1
CCSS.ELA-Literacy.W.6.1b
CCSS.ELA-Literacy.W.6.1
Skill: Explain "Argumentative Writing"

Grade Level: 5th-9th

Analogy: Martial Arts

Conversation: When you are having a debate or are expected to write an argumentative essay the most important thing to remember is that you must think like your opponent in order to win! In order to do this you must know how to explain very well so that your argument is protected. You must also be able to supply good examples for your thinking.

Example: In martial arts you have two people on a mat competing with each other. Opponents expect the kind of blow that their counter part may throw at him or her next. Because they expect it, they are better able to block and defend themselves. You must think like your opponent in order to win in sports and to win an argument!

Other ways to say Argument: disagreement, verbal war, debate

Essential Question: What kind of people argue for a living and get paid for it?

(On large white paper teacher creates an artifact in which students can respond to this question. Answers may include: lawyer, politician, doctor, detective, etc.)

Share: Allow students to share their thinking with the closest friend, and report out whole group upon your discretion. Post sticky notes on the large sheet of white paper and post it on the classroom wall as an artifact for future use.

Model: Show a video clip of students around the same grade level having a debate, or an argument. Students should be able to identify how each party had to "think like their opponent" in order to win the argument.

Independent Reflection: Have students reflect on the use of the skill alone. Students can write a short paragraph that elaborates on the essential question. Responses should include how this skill is beneficial in life and while writing. Responses should be used as an informal assessment, a teacher may choose to revisit and reteach parts of the lesson based on their findings.

Culminating Activity: *Give students a list of arguments to consider. Choose one with a friend, and have an in-class debate on the topic!*

"Activating Prior Knowledge"
"Argumentative Writing"
Career people who "argue" or have "verbal wars" in order to prove their case.
Lawyer
Doctor
"Get PAID To Argue for a living"

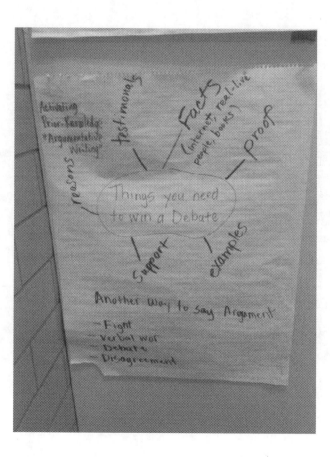

CCSS.ELA-Literacy.SL.6.1
CCSS.ELA-Literacy.RL.6.5
CCSS.ELA-Literacy.RL.6.10
Skill: Close Reading

Grade Level: 5th-9th

Analogy: Graffiti Artist

Conversation: Good readers read very closely and carefully to understand what they are reading. Some of the best readers even take notes in their head or on paper to connect to the text. In order to fully understand a text you must constantly give your self a purpose to keep on reading. This can be done by asking questions, making predictions, or just by considering your own thinking. When you do this it brings you closer and closer to the text, which helps you understand better!

Example: Have you ever been stuck by a train while you're in a car? As you are impatiently sitting there waiting for the train to move past you may sometimes notice the graffiti art that has been tagged on some of the train carts. Well, today when you closely read this text I want you to become that graffiti artist and tag your thinking all over the text that I give you!

Essential Question: How can "tagging" a text help you better understand it?

Share: Allow students to share their thinking with the closest friend, and report out whole group upon your discretion. Post sticky notes on the large sheet of white paper and post it on the classroom wall as an artifact for future use.

Model: Choose a high interest non-fiction text. Create a transparency for the text or article. Using an overhead projector model a close read while "tagging" the text with questions, predictions, and your own thinking. When you are done respond to authentic questions regarding your text selection!

Independent Reflection: Have students reflect on the use of the skill alone. Students can write a short paragraph that elaborates on the essential question. Responses should include how this skill is beneficial in life and while writing. Responses should be used as an informal assessment, a teacher may choose to revisit and reteach parts of the lesson based on their findings.

Close Reading

A close read means you will look very closely at a text in order to _fully_ understand it! _Good Readers_ use a combination of reading strategies to make sure they _understand_ what they're reading. This may include:

- Questioning
- Selective highlight
- Analyzing
- "tagging the text"
- Using context-clues
- Re-reading
- Thinking Aloud
- Connecting
- Visualizing

CCSS.ELA-Literacy.RL.6.2
CCSS.ELA-Literacy.RL.6.10
CCSS.ELA-Literacy.SL.6.1
Skill: Main Idea

Grade Level: 5th-9th

Analogy: Connecting the Dots!

Conversation: When you are trying to find the main idea of a text you need to read very closely. The main idea is what the text is mostly about. Every thing else would be considered a supporting detail! There are some helpful cue questions that you should think of when you are trying to identify the main idea. First, ask yourself what is the topic? Some people confuse the topic with the main idea! Second, ask yourself what about the topic is being expressed? This is the question that will lead you to the main idea. Lastly, ask yourself how can improve it? That's when you can go back into the text to find evidence/supporting details to prove you are right. Good readers simply connect the dots in reading to find the main idea! They will connect the thing that is mostly expressed with the details that support it.

Example: My mom doesn't feel well. She stayed up all night coughing, sneezing, and throwing up. Tomorrow my dad is going to take her to the doctor! (You may use your own example to make the connection)

Cues: **What is the topic?** Mom
    What about the topic is being expressed? Mom is sick
    How can improve this? She stayed up all night coughing, sneezing, etc
                  Dad will take her to the doctor

Essential Question: Why is being able to identify the main idea of a text so important?

Share: Allow students to share their thinking with the closest friend, and report out whole group upon your discretion. Post sticky notes on the large sheet of white paper and post it on the classroom wall as an artifact for future use.

Model: Choose a high interest non-fiction text. Create a transparency for the text or article. Using an overhead projector model a close read while "tagging" the text with questions, predictions, and your own thinking. When you are done respond to authentic questions regarding your text selection!

Independent Reflection: Have students reflect on the use of the skill alone. Students can write a short paragraph that elaborates on the essential question. Responses should include how this skill is beneficial while reading. Responses should be used as an informal assessment, a teacher may choose to revisit and reteach parts of the lesson based on their findings.

CCSS.ELA-Literacy.SL.6.1
CCSS.ELA-Literacy.RL.6.10
Skill: Questioning

Grade Level: 5th-9th

Analogy: A Talking Toddler

Conversation: Have you ever been around a toddler that is constantly talking about something. You try to stay interested and patient with them because you know they are just kids. Did you notice that these "talking toddlers" ask a whole bunch of questions! It seems that one question is always followed by another one, and another one! When you ask questions you gain understanding! That is what the toddler is trying to do. He or she is trying to understand the world around them.

Example: Good readers will constantly ask questions in their minds as they read to build understanding. The more you ask questions the more purposes you have for reading. Everyone wants to know if his or her question will be answered so that motivates you to keep reading.

Essential Question: Why is it important for readers to ask questions while they read? Why is it important to ask questions in life?

Share: Allow students to share their thinking with the closest friend, and report out whole group upon your discretion. Post sticky notes on the large sheet of white paper and post it on the classroom wall as an artifact for future use.

Model: Choose a high interest non-fiction or fiction text. Read it aloud to your group of students. You should model asking questions before, during, and after the text is read. Show students how this skill promotes understanding of what has been read.

Independent Reflection: Have students reflect on the use of the skill alone. Students can write a short paragraph that elaborates on the essential question. Responses should include how this skill is beneficial while reading and in life. Responses should be used as an informal assessment, a teacher may choose to revisit and re-teach parts of the lesson based on their findings.

CCSS.ELA-Literacy.SL.6.1
CCSS.ELA-Literacy.RL.6.5
CCSS.ELA-Literacy.RL.6.10
Skill: Synthesizing

Grade Level: 5th-9th

Analogy: Cool Concoctions or "Mirror, Mirror on the Wall"

Conversation: Have you ever made something that is special to you? It is your signature creation and it is something that you love and enjoy! Since you made it you understand what things you need in order to make it! Someone else wouldn't fully understand how to make it!

Example: When I was younger my siblings and I had contests on who could make the best tasting kool-aid! We all had our own special ingredients to make it just right! When you synthesize as you read it's like making a concoction in your head. Reading and occasionally stopping to think and develop news ideas or reflect on how you can improve something. In the case of reading, it's all about combining what you are reading about, with your ideas, in order to form new opinions and ideas.

Essential Question: How can reflecting or synthesizing help you to better understand what you are reading about? How can "synthesizing/reflection" personal choices help you to make better choices?

Share: Allow students to share their thinking with the closest friend, and report out whole group upon your discretion. Post sticky notes on the large sheet of white paper and post it on the classroom wall as an artifact for future use.

Model: Choose a high interest non-fiction text. Read it aloud to your group of students. You should model a think aloud that includes constant reflection. Teacher will use the evidence from the text combined with your new ideas, in order to develop a personal understanding of the text. Create an artifact on big paper to model thinking that divides text evidence, personal ideas, opinions, and/or a change of perspective. Show students how this skill promotes understanding of what has been read.

Independent Reflection: Have students reflect on the use of the skill alone. Students can write a short paragraph that elaborates on the essential question. Responses should include how this skill is beneficial while reading and in life. Responses should be used as an informal assessment, a teacher may choose to revisit and re-teach parts of the lesson based on their findings.

CCSS.ELA-Literacy.SL.6.1
CCSS.ELA-Literacy.RL.6.10
Skill: Visualizing

Grade Level: 5th-9th

Analogy: A picture paints a thousand words

Conversation: Have you ever listened to someone read you a story? Not just anyone, but someone who really reads well. They really jump into character and use just the right kind of expression to make the story really interesting! Their ability to read so well helps you to make images in your head! It's like a motion picture is playing inside your mind capturing all of the words that you are hearing being read to you! If this has ever happened to you that means you are a good listener but an even better reader!

Example: Have you ever heard the expression "A picture paints a thousand words?"

Essential Question: Why is it so important to visualize as you read?

Share: Allow students to share their thinking with the closest friend, and report out whole group upon your discretion. Post sticky notes on the large sheet of white paper and post it on the classroom wall as an artifact for future use.

Model: Read aloud a high-interest picture book. Allow students to sketch out images that they were able to visualize during the reading. Compare student images to the illustrator's images and discuss the similarities and differences.

Independent Reflection: Have students reflect on the use of the skill alone. Students can write a short paragraph that elaborates on the essential question. Responses should include how this skill is beneficial while reading and in life. Responses should be used as an informal assessment, a teacher may choose to revisit and re-teach parts of the lesson based on their findings.

Visualizing

Good readers are able to see as they read. This brings them in closer with the story, and allows them to paint *or text* a picture in their head. When you can do this you understand what you're reading better.

Another way to say it : Imagery

Title: Six dinner Sid

I say... (text)	I say... (my thinking)	(inference)
Sid lives at numbers 1, 2, 3, 4, 5, and 6 Aristotle places.	Why does Sid live in 6 different places?	Maybe he has 6 different owners

Title:
It says

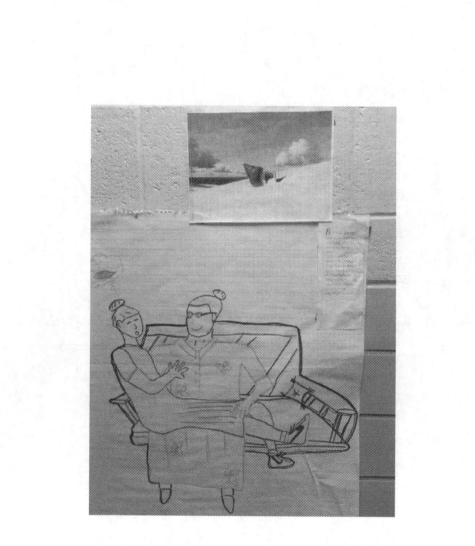

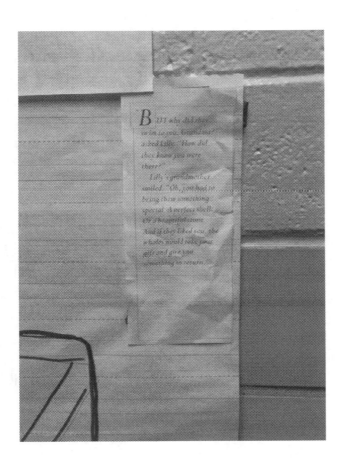

CCSS.ELA-Literacy.RL.6.1
CCSS.ELA-Literacy.SL.6.1
Skill: Activating Prior Knowledge (**Schema**)

Grade Level: 5th-9th

Analogy: An apple doesn't fall far from the tree

Conversation: Every person that walks this Earth comes from somewhere different and unique to them. Those environments determine what types of information gets downloaded into your brain cells. Since everyone has different experiences their exposures are also different and unique. This exposure can include a range of things. But, for the sake of school and academics lets limit exposures to books and vocabulary. Your unique experiences in life will help you understand the things we read, write, and talk about during school. However, everyone doesn't have the same experiences and won't be exposed to be same exact things as the next person. At times, you will have to give that person background knowledge in order to complete a task. Without establishing at background you will exclude some students from learning.

Example: A person who has been raised on a farm will have more experiences/ exposures to farm animals, produce, vegetation, etc. Therefore, when this type of learning presents itself in school that child will be able to tap into their prior-knowledge to comprehend the material.

Essential Question: Why is it important for children to have background knowledge before tackling challenges topics or subjects?

Share: Allow students to share their thinking with the closest friend, and report out whole group upon your discretion. Post sticky notes on the large sheet of white paper and post it on the classroom wall as an artifact for future use.

Model: Choose a high-interest topic along with corresponding texts to introduce to the class whole group. Pose a series of questions that would require a portion of the class to use background knowledge to answer, while the rest of the class struggles to answer the same questions. Discuss why some were equipped to answer while some were not. Explain to the class, that those who didn't have a Schema to pull from are now getting the background knowledge they lacked before the discussion began.

Independent Reflection: Have students reflect on the use of the skill alone. Students can write a short paragraph that elaborates on the essential question. Responses should include how this skill is beneficial while reading and in life. Responses should be used as an informal assessment, a teacher may choose to revisit and re-teach parts of the lesson based on their findings.

CCSS.ELA-Literacy.SL.6.1
Skill: Making Connections

Grade Level: 5th-9th

Analogy: Birds of a feather flock together

Conversation: Have you ever heard the expression "birds of a feather flock together?" Well, this expression basically means that people of the same experiences or interests tend to hang out together. When you think of that in an school/learning aspect, it just means the connections that you make while you read can build a strong relationship or understanding for what you are reading about. There are three types of connections good readers make while reading: Text to Text, Text to Self, or Text to World. Whenever, we make connections we are using our prior knowledge or experiences in life to make meaningful, authentic connections to the text.

Example: The key vocabulary word that should be used while making connections is: **remind**. Students should constantly ask these questions: What does this text **remind** you of? Does this text **remind** you of another text? Does this **remind** you of anything that happens in the real world?

Essential Question: Why is it important for students to try to make connections while they read? What could go wrong if students can't connect to a text their reading?

Share: Allow students to share their thinking with the closest friend, and report out whole group upon your discretion. Post sticky notes on the large sheet of white paper and post it on the classroom wall as an artifact for future use.

Model: Choose a high interest non-fiction or fiction text. Read it aloud to your group of students. You should model making authentic connections throughout the read aloud. It is very important to pre-select a book and align it to prior-experiences so that valid and authentic connections can be made. Show students how this skill promotes understanding of what has been read.

Independent Reflection: Have students reflect on the use of the skill alone. Students can write a short paragraph that elaborates on the essential question. Responses should include how this skill is beneficial while reading and in life. Responses should be used as an informal assessment, a teacher may choose to revisit and re-teach parts of the lesson based on their findings.

CCSS.ELA-Literacy.SL.6.1
Skill: Monitor and Clarify

Grade Level: 5th-9th

Analogy: If at first you don't succeed, dust yourself off and try again!

Conversation: Sometimes it takes people several times to attempt to do something before they finally get it right. It's no different than practicing your favorite sport. You will keep practicing hard until you reach your full potential. The goal is to use every trick you've got to make success happen for you.

Example: Whenever you get a piece of challenging text to read, you need to approach it just like it's your favorite sport. In order to succeed, you won't give up! You will use everything you've got to be successful, and if at first you don't succeed you will dust yourself off, reach way back in your "toolbox" and grab what you need to understand and tackle the text.

Essential Question: When students monitor and clarify as they're reading, why is it important to use a combination of reading skills to understand the text?

Share: Allow students to share their thinking with the closest friend, and report out whole group upon your discretion. Post sticky notes on the large sheet of white paper and post it on the classroom wall as an artifact for future use.

Model: Choose a high interest non-fiction or fiction text. Read it aloud to your group of students. You should model a range of decoding skills in order to understand technical vocabulary. In order to understand concepts, model using prior knowledge to connect to the text. It is very important to pre-select a book and align it to prior-experiences so that valid and authentic connections can be made. Show students how this skill promotes understanding of what has been read.

Independent Reflection: Have students reflect on the use of the skill alone. Students can write a short paragraph that elaborates on the essential question. Responses should include how this skill is beneficial while reading and in life. Responses should be used as an informal assessment, a teacher may choose to revisit and re-teach parts of the lesson based on their findings.

CCSS.ELA-Literacy.RI.6.5
CCSS.ELA-Literacy.SL.6.1
Skill: Text Structure

Grade Level: 5th-9th

Analogy: Built to last

Conversation: A structure is the way something is built. In order for an architect to build a structure they need to know the purpose it will serve. When an author writes a text, it's just like building a structure! First, the author figures out a purpose for building a text. Then, the way they use their words will structure their writing. When we really look closely at the way a text is built, we tend to understand it better.

Example: When a person is familiar with the design of something they become more comfortable with it. For example, if you've been living in the same house for ten years, and you suddenly have a power outage although it's dark in your house you'd probably be able to navigate in the dark successfully because you are comfortable with the design or structure of your home. When you become comfortable with the different techniques that authors use when they structure a text, you begin to understand what you're reading much better.

Essential Question: How can the ways an author builds a text, impact what you understand?

Why is text structure important for non-fiction reading?

Share: Allow students to share their thinking with the closest friend, and report out whole group upon your discretion. Post sticky notes on the large sheet of white paper and post it on the classroom wall as an artifact for future use.

Model: Choose a high interest text or a content area textbook for students to examine. Allow students to refer to an artifact or poster that has signal words or phrases that would lead them in the direction of a particular type of writing. For example, if a type of text is structured around cause and effect, the reader may notice words or key phrases like: for this reason, as a result, consequently, etc.

Independent Reflection: Have students reflect on the use of the skill alone. Students can write a short paragraph that elaborates on the essential question. Responses should include how this skill is beneficial while reading and in life. Responses should be used as an informal assessment, a teacher may choose to revisit and re-teach parts of the lesson based on their findings.

CCSS.ELA-Literacy.RL.6.5
CCSS.ELA-Literacy.RL.6.4
CCSS.ELA-Literacy.SL.6.1
Skill: Context Clues

Grade Level: 5th-9th

Analogy: Reading between the Lines

Conversation: Today I want to step into your world. I know that you guys have a hidden language that you use with only your friends and family. Most people call it "slang." You guys have created your own words, and each word represents another word that is standard in he English language. It's actually pretty cool and genius! Today I'll use context clues to figure out what your slang words really mean!

Example: Ask one student to share out a "slang word." To illustrate a sample word may be "swagg."

Mr. Thomas has crazy swagg. Look at his shoes, they're so nice!

Interpretation: Mr. Thomas has great style. Look at his shoes, they're so nice!

Context Clues: look at his shoes, they're so nice

Essential Question: How can words that surround an unfamiliar word help you figure out what the unknown word means?

Why is it important to use context clues when reading?

Share: Allow students to share their thinking with the closest friend, and report out whole group upon your discretion. Post sticky notes on the large sheet of white paper and post it on the classroom wall as an artifact for future use.

Model: Choose a high interest text or a content area textbook for students to examine. Allow students to read portions of the text that contain big words. Students should practice using context clues to gain meaning. Generate a list of possible synonyms and discuss with a partner until a consensus is made.

Independent Reflection: Have students reflect on the use of the skill alone. Students can write a short paragraph that elaborates on the essential question. Responses should include how this skill is beneficial while reading and in life. Responses should be used as an informal assessment, a teacher may choose to revisit and reteach parts of the lesson based on their findings.

Who wants to use a pencil over an iPad?

"Bringing Authentic Writing Back Into The Classroom in Relatable Ways"

Most kids don't want to write their names on a sheet of paper, so what on Earth makes us think that would want to write anything that requires actual thought?

It's funny to hear teachers complain about a student's inability to write because most of the teachers who do the complaining were not writers themselves when they were students. The question then becomes:

How can a teacher make writing appealing to students if they're not really fond of writing either?

As educators we must constantly remind ourselves that the only thing that will ever be constant, is change. Traditional methods of writing have changed, but some of our veteran teachers are living in constant denial instead of constant change. The teaching profession is always changing! It seems like this would be a concept that we should be comfortable with by now. The truth is, change will shock your system before your mindset starts to accept the fact that something different is actually going to happen.

There will be very few occasions when you will be able to successfully grab a student's attention in writing with the traditional paper and pencil tactics. The transition is complete. Our children have graduated from the pen to the computer or iPad! Although, I feel that using computerized devices such as those to write essays or various writing assignments robs students of acquiring useful writing skills, and makes children lazy due to spell check, dictionary and thesaurus check, and all of the other convenient features that these technical devices offer. Most of us need to just get over it and decide to invest our energy into the most contemporary writing practices that will engage students in ways that will make writing both relatable and enjoyable.

Let us consider what our urban youth is exposed to on a daily basis. Music in my opinion may be on the top of the list. Each genre of music is an expression of art. The diversity found in urban schools embraces all types of music, actually making each child a well-rounded individual that may develop very few biases. From my observations, I've found that this generation is more willing to accept things that are different and appreciate those differences for what they are. Students are listening to music that crosses color lines and barriers. These genres include: hip-hop, r&b, pop, alternative, rock, rap, etc.)

Our students are smart enough to analyze the meanings of song lyrics to gain understanding. This proves that they are more than capable of producing written work that is well within the spectrum of learning and comfort.

Motivation is born by beginning in the students "comfort zone." When students feel accepted on their own terms, a trust develops. This trust eventually ignites a confidence. Once their confidence is nurtured and appreciated by teachers, students will confidently begin to step outside of their comfort zones in order try new things.

Our children are also exposed to a plethora of technology. Technology has rapidly graduated from pagers to cellular phones, desktop to laptop computers, now we have iPads!! We've gone from cassette tapes to cds, vhs tapes to DVDs. Now most of everything we desire is only a download away.

What kid do you know that would readily be excited to use a pencil and sheet of paper when there are so many other exciting outlets to use! Unless teachers make the concept of writing exciting and relatable, trying to get children to write would be just as exciting as watching paint dry. Children must be inspired to write, and this inspiration needs to be just as constant as "change."

Technology must be included in the modern process of writing in order to inspire children to write. However, for the security of not enabling our student's, technology should be a give and take relationship in the classroom. The expectation for students to know how to produce meaningful and authentic writing on paper should never go away. Instead, it should coexist within the system of the writing process that includes both traditional and modern writing practices. Teachers may decide to customize their writing process/system as they see fit in order to expose children to the wide array of technology that can be used for their writing, while still showing the significance of the "Shakespearean" style of writing.

The next several lesson plans will demonstrate how some of our most traditional genres of writing can be altered in order to spark an interest for writing, while motivating children to want to write! I will take a look at the following genres:

- Persuasive Writing
- Poetry Analysis
- Argumentative Writing
- Expository Writing
- Free Writing
- Blogs

CCSS.ELA-Literacy.W.6.2e
CCSS.ELA-Literacy.SL.6.1
Genre: Persuasive Writing

Grade Level: 5th-9th

Analogy: What's in it for me?

Questions to ponder over:

- What kinds of people make a living by persuading other people?
- What outside sources in the world can you find different examples of persuasion?
- How can persuasion be beneficial to some kinds of people?
- What is the difference between persuasion and manipulation?

IDEA 1

Ignite an interest:
(conversation piece)

"Convince me"

Being able to persuade is an art form. Everyone can't do it. That's why everyone isn't a lawyer, car salesman, or real estate agent to say the least. It takes a very special talent to be able to convince another person to do something different. Most of these artists have studied different tactics in order to be able to successfully persuade another person into doing something. Can anyone think of a tactic that is used to persuade? (If valid answers are given GREAT, if not start generating your own list on a large sheet of paper that could be used as an artifact in the classroom after the introduction of the lesson.)

<u>**Introduce tactics**</u>

Emotional appeal: (guilt, charm, bribe, threat/fear) encourage students to tap into an emotion in order to persuade

Testimonial: share a fictional/non-fictional account that taps into an emotion in order to persuade

Bandwagon: mention all of the important people/places who have adopted what you are selling

Go for it: Allow students to choose one of the tactics listed above. Have students write a short paragraph persuading the audience of their choice into doing something. Remember, this is just for fun! Students should find enjoyment in writing first before expectations for persuasive writing become more procedural.

IDEA 2

Ignite an interest:
(conversation piece)

"Letter to the Principal"

"Today I want you to write a letter to our principal. Imagine this: you have an opportunity to persuade the principal into inviting a celebrity speaker into our school. This celebrity could be anyone you want it to be. However, there will only be one winner. The student who is able to "convince" the principal through their writing why their celebrity should be the one chosen will get to announce to the entire student body who the guest speaker will be."

Go for it: Remind students this is not really going to happen and it is only to inspire their best writing. You may choose to share the writing with the principal to gain moral support throughout the process of writing.

IDEA 3

Ignite an interest:
(conversation piece)

"Parent/Child Script"

"Most of you all love to act, role play, or be a part of a funny skit. Today I want you to choose one partner to work with to develop a skit between a parent and a child. Once you choose your partner you can flip a coin to decide who will be who. The goal of the skit is to write a script of persuasion conversation. (Each group is given a teenage situation on a slip of paper) these scenarios should be pre-selected. Whoever the child is in the script must find a way to convince the parent into allowing the "given" situation to happen. The listening audience will make a decision whether or not the child did a good job persuading the parent." (identify the tactics that were being used)

Go for it: Remind students that this activity is just a warm-up to inspire their best writing. Students should be expected to follow a more technical process for writing persuasively after they've gained enough confidence.

CCSS.ELA-Literacy.SL.6.1
CCSS.ELA-Literacy.W.6.2e
CCSS.ELA-Literacy.RL.6.5
Genre: Poetic Analysis

Grade Level: 5th-9th

Analogy: Optical Illusions allow you to see things differently

Questions to ponder over:

- Why do you think you can get multiple meanings out of the same poem?
- How does description play a role in reading and writing poetry?
- How significant is a person prior-knowledge when trying to understand poetry?
- What do you think the outcome of reading a poem should be?

IDEA

Ignite an interest:
(conversation piece)

"What you see is not always what you get"

"I'd like to show you a picture of what you call an "optical illusion." (*the teacher should have pre-selected a picture of an optical illusion for students to view*)

"I want you to study the picture intently and on a scratch sheet of paper write down what you see, but don't say it out loud, and don't let anyone see what you wrote." (*the optical illusion that you should have selected should contain an image that shows more than one thing*)

"Choose a partner, and reveal what you found in the optical illusion to each other. Did you both see the same things?" (*If not, show both images to the children*)

Answer the following question:

How are optical illusions and interpretations of poems alike?
(record student responses on a big-sheet of paper)
Go for it: Encourage students to write a personal poem of their choice. Students may choose to share their poem with a friend. Friends should attempt to interpret the poem, and have their poetic analysis confirmed by their partner.

Remind students that this activity is just a warm-up to inspire their best writing. Students should be expected to follow a more technical process for writing poetry after they've gained enough confidence.

CCSS.ELA-Literacy.SL.6.1
CCSS.ELA-Literacy.W.6.1
CCSS.ELA-Literacy.W.6.2e
CCSS.ELA-Literacy.W.6.1b
CCSS.ELA-Literacy.W.6.1d

Genre: Argumentative

Grade Level: 5th-9th

Analogy: A martial artist must think like their opponent in order to win

Questions to ponder over:

- What kind of careers can you think of where people have to argue to prove their case?
- What are other ways to say argue?
- Are arguments always hostile in nature?
- How can thinking like your opponent help you win an argument?

IDEA

Ignite an interest:
(conversation piece)

"Hah-yah"

"When you are having a debate or are expected to write an argumentative essay the most important thing to remember is that you must think like your opponent in order to win! In order to do this you must know how to explain very well so that your argument is protected. You must also be able to supply good examples for your thinking. In martial arts you have two people on a mat competing with each other. Opponents expect the kind of blow that their counter part may throw at him or her next. Because they expect it, they are better able to block and defend themselves. You must think like your opponent in order to win in sports and to win an argument!

❖ **Introduce vocabulary pertinent to the lesson**

Go for it: As a whole group generate a list of arguments that are appealing to the age-range in your classrooms. These arguments should include current popular trends that affect student behaviors on a daily basis. For example:

- Schools uniforms should be banned

- Violent video games should be banned

- Students should have the right to text during school hours

- Old school pencils are more reliable than mechanical pencils

- Teachers should receive quarterly report cards from students

- School administrators should have no right to invade student lockers allowing us the right to our privacy

- Students should have the right to answer 3 calls on their cell phones per school day

Upon completing a **controversial** list of topics students should be separated into groups that defend their desired position.

Students should be able to incorporate their own thinking with research found in various sources that will help them to defend their argument. Use the next several days to draft arguments. (Teachers follow their own process of writing for fine-tuning) **Culminating Activity:** Class Debates

CCSS.ELA-Literacy.SL.6.1
CCSS.ELA-Literacy.W.6.2
CCSS.ELA-Literacy.W.6.3c
CCSS.ELA-Literacy.W.6.2e
CCSS.ELA-Literacy.W.6.2d
Genre: Expository

Grade Level: 5th-9th

Analogy: Show & Tell

Questions to ponder over:

- How can reading non-fiction help people?
- Why is it more helpful to demonstrate what you are trying to explain?
- What makes a person an expert at something?
- What are the benefits of reading an expository essay?

IDEA

Ignite an interest:
(conversation piece)

"Demonstration Speech w/visual props"

"Our entire world operates through non-fiction sources. While fictional genres help us escape our realities for brief amounts of time, the significance of non-fiction will always reign supreme. In order to be in constant connection with what goes on in the real world will must be informed by non-fiction materials or sources."

"Expository writing and reading is our invitation to join the informational highway. Being able to explain anything in great length means that you must be somewhat of an expert in that area of your life. The more informational texts you read, the more knowledge you'll be able to regurgitate or spit out!"

"However, when you can actually demonstrate what you're explaining, you will be able to help other people learn what you are trying to communicate even better! That is why we will combine word choice with demonstration in order to explain how to do something."

Go for it: Introduce vocabulary that is essential to writing an expository. For example, transitional words of phrases that show time-order sequence, description, comparison, or cause and effect. A teacher may want to produce a generic version of some of the most commonly used transitional phrases and post it on large paper in a visible area in the classroom.

Have students individually jot down things that they can do well. Remind students that they must consider themselves experts in all of their choices. Students should choose at least three things. After they have selected three, allow them to pick the best one out of three. Students should complete a graphic organizer or an outline in order to explain how to do "their chosen topic."

Materials: Encourage students to gather visuals or props at home in order to demonstrate in front of the entire classroom. Create a scoring rubric that combines the oral effort, with the demonstration effort.

Provide adequate amount of time for students to write their process. Upon completing the written portion of the assignment, students should be given enough time to rehearse their process, and demonstrate their process simultaneously.

Remind students that this activity is just a warm-up to inspire their best writing. Students should be expected to follow a more technical process for writing an expository essay after they've gained enough confidence.

(Encourage students to choose topics that are culturally different, so the diversity within the classroom can learn from one another)

❖ *One of the best demonstration speeches I witnessed was done by one of my Asian students who taught everyone in the classroom how to use chopsticks correctly. He brought in enough chopsticks for everyone, and enough white rice for everyone to practice with.*

CCSS.ELA-Literacy.W.6.2e
CCSS.ELA-Literacy.W.6.4
Genre: Free Writing

Grade Level: 5th-9th

Analogy: The best things in life are Free!

Questions to ponder over:

- Why do you think most kids hate writing?
- If you could write about anything you wanted, what would it be?
- Do you think some of your favorite singers, rappers, or musicians are good at writing? Why? Or, Why not?
- How can you connect emotions to writing?

IDEA

Ignite an interest:
(conversation piece)

"It is what it is"

"There is no better feeling you can get than from telling someone you care about a little bit about yourself. Not only does it make your relationship stronger, but it also invites another person to make an emotional connection to you too. Emotions are one of the truest things there are in this world, why not share them with people so that you can become better understood!"

Go for it: Read aloud a personal composition of something you wrote specifically for this assignment. Your composition should be personal, authentic, and your words should tap into an emotion. Decide prior to your writing this, what emotion you want the class to feel and what you're comfortable sharing. Discussion should follow, and this would be a great time to allow students to answer the questions above.

Independent: Tell students to choose an emotion, and think of things they are comfortable with sharing with the class or you. Encourage students to write about anything they want to share. This is a "free" write. Give students the option of reading their composition aloud, or turning it in quietly to you. Regardless of their choice, their writing should receive the same respect as those who chose to share by reading it out loud.

❖ *You may want to encourage students to keep a daily diary or journal to let their emotions out on a daily basis. Explain to students this is a healthy way to manage stress.*

CCSS.ELA-Literacy.W.6.4
CCSS.ELA-Literacy.W.6.6
Genre: Writing Blogs

Grade Level: 5th-9th

Analogy: Who needs Facebook?

Questions to ponder over:

- Why is facebook fun for teenagers?
- If you could create a facebook webpage for school what would some of your rules for using it be?
- Does writing on social media websites make you feel more comfortable with writing in general? Why or Why not?

IDEA

Ignite an interest:
(conversation piece)

"Schoolbook"

"Social media has become very popular over the years. It allows people to become cyber friends, voice their opinions on different issues, stay informed about celebrity news, world news, and is overall, an outlet for expression. Blogs allow you to express yourself with no consequence of being judged on sentence structure, or if all of your subjects and verbs agree with each other. It's comfortable! It's free! And, it invites you to be yourself."

"Now, what if I told you that we are going to create our own version of social-media for classroom use only! Our blogs would be focused on writing, but with everyone will have the freedom of expression. We would have to establish healthy guidelines for use, but no student will ever get marked down for grammatical and spelling errors."

Materials: computers, IPads, Internet access, teacher webpage

Go for it: Discuss the rules and expectations of blogging with students. Upon completion of an assigned reading, post a question of the webpage for students. Students should engage in conversation that both answers the question and responds to other peers that are answering the same question. This activity creates a comfortable atmosphere for communicating answers and analyzing the answers of others.

Blogs can be created as a response to literature in any content setting. This allows students, teachers, and parents the ability to chime in on discussions or simply monitor student progress in an informal way.

Essential Questions

1.

2.

3.

4.

Reflection

Choose 1 of the essential questions to elaborate on. How is this skill useful in reading and in life? Give specific examples to prove your understanding.

How is our reading strategy important to our education and how can it affect our lives in the real world? Use the bullets below to give examples.

Education

-
-
-
-
-

Real World

-
-
-
-
-

Cut and place each strip in a bag. Shake up bag and allow groups to pull a reading strategy out. Plan a skit that will fit the strategy that was pulled and act it out whole group. Those watching should be able to identify your reading strategy based on what you included in your performance!

PREDICTING

INFERRING

QUESTIONING

CLARIFYING

CAUSE & EFFECT

SUMMARIZING

CONTEXT CLUES
ANALYZING
EVALUATION
CLOSE READING
VISUALIZING
MONITOR & CLARIFY
MAKING CONNECTIONS

MAIN IDEA				

Title:

Author:

How many times did you use each strategy as you read? Use tally marks to record how many times you were actively engaged in the text by using one of the following thinking skills.

PREDICT	INFER	QUESTION	MAKE A CONNECTION	VISUALIZE

How did using those thinking skills help deepen your understanding of what you read?

Desk Jeopardy

Summarizing	Inferring	Main Idea	Context Clues	Analyzing
100	100	100	100	100
200	200	200	200	200

300	300	300	300	300
400	400	400	400	400
500	500	500	500	500
600	600	600	600	600
700	700	700	700	700

❖ Teachers may personalize questions that reinforce each reading comprehension skill. Questions may be pulled directly from curriculum instruction, book studies, literature circle activities, etc.

The Week in Retrospect

Reading:

Analogy to Real World:

What went well?

Things to reconsider:

Additions:

Did any Authentic Conversations come up?

Writing:

Analogy to Real World:

What went well?

Things to reconsider:

Additions:

Did any Authentic Conversations come up?

Draw yourself as an adult in the career choice of your dreams.

List the skills you will need to be proficient in while in and outside of school to accomplish your dream career above:

My name is _____

I am in _____ grade.

My Reflection On Reading

Favorite book:

Most used phrase:

A slang word that I use a lot:

Translation for that word:

Favorite genre of reading:

The book that I remember the most as a child:

What made the book so special?

I enjoy/don't enjoy reading because............

In order to become a better reader you must...........

Sometimes I struggle when I read because.............

Favorite Author:

Favorite song:

A nursery rhyme that I remember is:

Because...........

Would you rather read or write?

What do you think reading and writing have in common?

Do you plan on attending college?

(Use the following responses that you provided to create a poster board presentation of your background in reading, and be prepared to share in class)

Materials: (tri-fold poster board, coloring utensils, scissors, glue, pictures, etc.)

Conclusion

Motivation is by far the magic ingredient for successfully getting students interested in reading. The world in which we live in is constantly evolving, with technology being at the forefront of any and every new venture as it relates to education, profession, or daily living. Our children live in a world where it takes more than what it took traditionally to keep them motivated. As educators we must step out of our comfort zones and step into character in order to demand the attention of our students. The character you choose to jump into should change often, because there will always be something more captivating and innovative for children to turn to instead of textbooks and boring curriculum expectations.

As much as students complain about having order in their life, I've learned that they accept it rather well when it is consistent and welcoming. Students love to have some control in their environment. Once students are accustomed to routines within the classroom setting whether it is behavioral or academic, students become interested in heading up roles that will help maintain the order in the classroom.

Without motivation being at the core of learning, any attempt to get children involved in academics would be profitless. If children are uninspired at school, even if they are highly capable of producing quality work, chances are some would still choose not to do so. In an effort to compete with technology, classroom teachers need to embrace the kind of creativity that will connect content with the relevance of an individuals experiences, consistently research the most efficient methods of teaching and learning, and classroom teachers must teach subjects that they are truly passionate about. The transfer of energy is very real, and if teachers are not enthused and energetic about what they are trying to convey there is no way the students would want to hold on to the message, to them, it is just as insignificant as the teacher has made it sound. A salesman is only as good as his pitch and his product! We are all trying to get children to buy into education. Therefore, we must perfect our pitch!

Printed in the United States
By Bookmasters